DECISION, TRUMP, THE GOP, AND THE EVANGELICALS

2024 ELECTION

DECISION, TRUMP, THE GOP, AND THE EVANGELICALS

2024 ELECTION

Politics, Poetry and Prose

ANDRAE POWELL

To order additional copies of this book, contact:
Xlibris
844-714-8691
www.Xlibris.com
Orders@Xlibris.com
859217

Contents

PART II

Poems, Politics, and Prose

Also by Andrae Powell

Poems of Inspiration, Love, and Spirituality.
COVID Politics and Prose.

Introduction

The extent to which Donald Trump and his allies are willing to double talk, continuously stretch themselves to circumvent the law and find excuses to prop up the former president is mind-blowing. It displays a picture of desperation and a mentality averse and antagonistic to American leadership and governance.

"DECISION, TRUMP, THE GOP, AND THE EVANGELICALS" 2024 Election is a preface to an in-depth study of Donald Trump and the MAGA movement, their influence, and their legacy in American politics during the Trump era (2016–2024 and beyond).

Trump—seemingly unaware of the bounds and restraints of modern political discourse, presidential awareness, and protocol—continues to make a mockery of the presidential calling. The Republican leadership fails to upbraid his missteps and failings—and they make no bones about the fact that they would continue to tolerate the former president's endless shenanigans.

As the American electorate meets on Tuesday, November 5, 2024, to vote and decide their future—and the lives of their children and grandchildren—they should appreciate this unique and amazing American state, what it has stood for, its great legacy, history, resourcefulness, abundance and the unending blessings that have been bestowed upon it.

This could only come from a God who has chosen this

American soil to display his glory and grace, extending his favor and blessing to the second arm of the root of Jesse, the father of David, of the lineage of Jesus Christ. What other explanation is there for the continued record-breaking unemployment and positive growth of the United States? Its strong economy is driven by industries, manufacturing, business, trade, services, real estate, consumer spending, and confidence. Is a Q4 GDP growth above 3 percent normal? it is not. The country's population is more than 331.9 million, and the unemployment rate is less than 5 percent. Almost every eligible, healthy, able-bodied person in the United States is gainfully employed to better themselves, their families, and their loved ones. This is totally amazing. The abundance and prosperity are extensive, and many Americans need to give thanks, count their many blessings, and appreciate their good fortune, the United States and what it stands for. There are social and economic ills, yes, addiction, homelessness and crime. Corrective measures have been put in place to mitigate these issues, nevertheless, the American economy is robust and productive.

In the midst of this abundance in 2024, it boggles the mind how Trump, a political outsider and newcomer, in a political sense—who was once a Democrat—has been able to test, manipulate and expose the fickleness of the Republican Party and its leadership, normalizing the premium value of the presidency. In these so-called modern, enlightened times, how can the Republican Party be so boxed in on all sides, muzzled, surrendering and submitting to the person and the personage of Donald Trump and what his character represents. Is Trump a strongman or a strongman in the making, is he the type of leader America needs now, one who buddy up and idolize shady dictators who have no respect for human life or human rights? Trump, a personality and character that have attracted indictable offences and displayed felonious attitudes, should he again be awarded the presidential seal of approval?

Since Trump took office in 2016, the pillars of the Constitution and its guardrails don't seem to matter anymore. The Democrats seem to be the party that favors integrity, purpose, direction, anti-chaos, principles and the rule of Law.

Trump has changed the GOP and has completely revolutionized the cultural ethos of the Republican Party from one of policy, intellectual discourse, constitutionalism, and conservatism to one of Trumpism, culture wars, nationalism, name-calling, conflicts, hate mongering and personality politics.

America's most pressing issue is its demise of its own making, the ripping apart of its fundamental ideals from within, and its divisiveness and inability to synchronize its differences and exist as a unit. The unique qualities of the American state and the American Constitution speak volumes about the government. This country, the United States of America was formulated in the mind of an eternal, wise God—not to be torn apart and trampled upon by careless mortals.

The Trump Battle: The Election Lie "Fighting Donald Trump's Battle is to live in Trump's Mind"

With hardheadedness as tough as nails and zero counsel or advice about a strategy on moving forward after losing the 2020 election, Trump—in his capacity as an elder statesman—chose to fight a losing battle by continuing to beat a dead horse by claiming that the 2020 election was stolen. It is no surprise that Trump chose to take this renegade course of action. The natural tendency after losing a race is to feel disappointed, vanquished, defeated, and dissatisfied. However, through all the disappointments, we remain fully hinged and can give account that all our screws are in the right place. We are not so embittered by our loss that it consumes our very existence, lashing out in every direction, spewing threats at the opposition, hate like leaches sucking our brains.

The normal, balanced, and levelheaded thing for Trump to do would be to lay low and, take some quality time out to process and put into perspective his election loss, for the sake of Democracy, the American Constitution, and the American people. He could have, present his case to the American populace or pursued other options that are available. American voters would have taken into account this seemingly humble, wise, and bold move, which could have added merit to his stature as a former president. The electorate would undoubtedly take note of his wisdom and political acumen, adding political and voting credit to the Trump brand. His future prospects and outlook would be refined and refreshing. The reset could have advanced his political future.

Instead, the surprising and continuing damage Trump chose to engage in (typical Trump) with the aiding and abetting of his myopic political allies, tried to capsize the American Democratic system, the foundation and root of American socio-political stability. Despite how strong-willed and determined he is, American Democracy stood firm. The American democratic system of government did not bow to the Trump cult or Trump's nationalism efforts. The stubborn, twice impeached and convicted former president can't stop adding fuel to the fire of lies about a stolen election or backing down from his frivolous claims about the 2020 election. He has already started digging himself an asinine hole, which continues to break out into a political pit, in every way, politically, legislatively, and judicially. To back down or back off from these preposterous claims would mean more pain of defeat, political embarrassment, and mental agony, moreover, his double-down strategy won't let him stop inciting the American democracy takedown madness. Trump's mind is not wired to live to fight another day, it's either to win or lose dirty and nastily, then crash and burn down the whole house.

The strategy employed by Trump, it seems is, trying some type of psychological wizardry. He has mentally blindfolded his supporters and successful pulled the claim of a fraudulent election over their eyes and minds. Relating to a poem that was written with a sarcastic tint, (Don, Don't Throw it All Away) the Poet implored and beseeched the Donald to make the best of his presidency. Trump, in his twilight years, whether he wants to believe it or not, gets one shot at the presidency, the same as all other presidents. They can either hit the target and get it right or lose and bow out. If the target is missed in the first term, it would be difficult to secure a second term. All presidents are aware of this fact, that's why losing presidents exit the race after their first term loss and do not run a second time, especially if they have a blemished and questionable first term in office.

On the chilly morning of January 17, 2016, Trump stood with his right hand on the Bible and took the oath of office. By then, many people had already made predictions about his presidency. Despite the many clamoring, great expectations and predictions, no one could have thought, or dreamed that after four short years as President, Trump would actually incite an insurrection against America to try to overturn the 2020 election, which he lost to Joe Biden.

His atrocious and diabolic acts, trying to convince the unconvinced, throwing dirty water, lies, and stains on the American electoral system had borne some very bitter fruits. He discredited and tarnished the American electoral process, dogged, trashed, and smeared the American Democracy.

The Republican Party that once espoused and adopted high moral principles, honored constitutionalism, and Evangelical Christian ideals, many now think it almost impossible to believe that this Trumpian scheme and con gamesmanship introduced to the once-grand Republican brand, could have taken root and flourished in the Evangelically enlightened GOP.

When Trump started to spew the Big Lie, it was unfortunate that few stood up to call a spade a spade, even when the snowballing effects were obvious. At the time, the election lie seemed like a "meal ticket" and it was an attractive, financially lucrative, and rewarding path for the senators and leadership of the Republican Party, they all bought and sold the Big Lie as a legitimate election talking point. The party of Lincoln and Reagan had been solidly bewitched and had fallen from grace and the high principles of former Republicans. The current crop of party leaders has chosen to drug and suffocate their consciences with a Trumpian concoction of lies, smokescreens, and conspiracy theories. Trump's cheerleaders in the Republican hierarchy, put on blinders, lockstep and fell in line behind him as he continued to sing his election blues from the White House to Mar-a-Lago.

Lucifer instigated a rebellion against godly authority, but he was only able to pull one-third of the angels from the heavenly realms of glory. Donald Trump was more successful than Lucifer, who instigated a rebellion against godly authority. Trump was able to outsmart, the entire hierarchy of the GOP and pull them to the cultlike schism of Trumpism, diminishing the traditional values, beliefs, and basic Republican principles. In comparison, Lucifer failed to inspire less than one third of the heavenly host to a state of ungrateful rebellion. I assume the hierarchy of angelic intelligent beings would act differently and be less easily persuaded to engage in an act of hostility, malice, and political cannibalism. Trump had a greater success rate than Lucifer, "the Beelzebub." Trump was the instigator and whip that triggered the failed uprising and insurrection against the American democratic system, his own government, and the system of free and fair elections. Trump was the first president of the United States to engage and incite an insurrection. This title and actions are of little or no consequence to Trump, he believes his actions were justified. He thinks he has presidential immunity and therefore he should not be held accountable for any his actions.

If these political actions by Trump were played out by another ethnicity, race, or political group, it would have been more consequential. There would have been much more heat and retribution for the perpetrators, perhaps an all-out war, instead, he was given free pass to obliterate and assault the United States Capitol. Lives were lost, mental and physical trauma was inflicted upon many people during this dark period in America's history. Many people suffered life-threatening wounds, both security forces and civilians, without much of a consequence or bearing some form of responsibility. If he could instigate an insurrection on America's most valued institutions, with lives, property, and the American Constitution at stake, there is no doubt, given a second opportunity he would wreak havoc, trample the system for his own glory, and enact revenge to save his own skin and fragile ego.

In the present scenario in which Trump has found himself,

in which other comprehensive moving parts, political and legal, are integral and revolves around him, as was the Jan. 6 revolt, in the today's political climate, sustained thought and extensive analysis and evaluation are required, Trump will most definitely short circuit himself. The simple reason is, he does not care about analytics, evaluations, and the outcome of events, or long-term effects. His often-used defense mechanisms will kick into gear, predictably taking things personally, if he can't get his way, he will throw verbal, psychological petrol or encourage others to do it for him. He will fight psychological warfare, do the name calling tactic, denigrate the character of others, blow whistles and self-destruct.

As he singlehandedly nearly triggers the collapse of the American democracy, the Judicial system gives him privileged pass and the right to tear apart the system and do as he pleases in the name of Presidential immunity. In 1788, the founding fathers established the electoral college to elect a president. Since then, it has been part of the American democratic process and a sure bet for fair and honest elections. This, an excellent accomplishment. Thanks to Trump, Americans can no longer tell other countries how to do things. Americans can no longer demonstrate how to democratically elect a president or a leader in a free and fair election. America has lost its credibility, political clout, and authority as the standard bearers of Democracy. This is without a doubt a crying shame, the once forceful crusader of Democracy. These are serious indictments on the facilitators, co-conspirators, and the yes men of Donald Trump against the American State.

With words of distortion, misrepresentation, and impishness, Trump and his co-conspirators repeatedly have stabbed at the heart of the American electoral system. Few cried foul, the GOP and the right cheered him on, and the liberal left sat silent while he wreaked havoc and did irreversible damage to American democracy. It was blatant political desecration, shredding the Constitution, the very foundation on which American democracy was built.

Sir Walter Scott said, "Oh what a tangled web we weave, when at first, we practice to deceive"

(A Sir Walter Scott's phrase, certainly laid it all bare in words) Trump's attempts to bankrupt and make a mockery of the American Democratic system, will stain American politics for decades to come. American Democracy, no longer the hallmark and emblem of western civilization or the gold standard of electoral success, favoring fair play over dictatorship and chaos, truth and justice over lies, political gamesmanship, civility, decorum and social advancement over racism, hatred and bigotry.

Trump's Charismatic and Magnetic Personality

Trump, the novice and uncouth rookie politician has managed to deter and dissuade men and women you thought were role models, standard bearers, career politicians and senators who have given years of sterling service to the nation and the Constitution. Men and women who many Americans thought were lawmakers, senators or bold politicians who you thought would be ready to take a stand to defend the Constitution and American Democracy, to at least speak up and safeguard the Constitution from treason and political breaches. The political right now seems to have dismissed their oaths and pledges and have been cornered and tongue tied by Trump, surrendering their reputation for political crumbs that fall from table of Trumpism. Men who are baked in the system of American Governance, who have practiced and claimed to know and respect American laws and the Constitution, wilt and buckled rather than stand up for truth and integrity. Law makers who had greased and kept the wheels of justice turning, trembled and bowed to Trump's whims and fancy. Republicans who you thought were elected, placed as stewards and defenders of the United States Constitution, who solemnly swore to support and defend the Constitution, to bear true faith and allegiance. They like stubble and wimps cast aside their garments of truth and justice and wallowed in Trump's swampy morass and concoctions of lies. They continue to choose Trump over love of country, giving half-baked lip service to American laws and the Constitution. They oscillate between right and wrong and truth and lies. The United States Constitution and their consciences. They go back on their words and bend backward to accommodate stupidity and absurdity, Trump doesn't care about their measly offerings and personal sacrifices. They suck up for sucking up sake. Their tales of woe and personal challenges are of no consequence to Trump. Their political effort to upend the 2020 election result have left many of his supporters mired in debt, unending litigations, personal bankruptcy and imprisonment. Trump will praise you today and damn you tomorrow.

We must admit, Trump is a masterpiece, a business and political icon, he is a national treasure. I love Trump, he is funny, smart, charismatic, and magnetic, but that does not insulate him from criticism. His personality demands from people as they are willing to give. He requires an unspoken and nonverbal contract of loyalty which seldom reciprocate in equal measure.

If you truly understand him, he is a great guy. Without his neediness, childlike cravings for admiration. Trump would be a great leader. He almost is the perfect white hope for these postmodern times. He would be the one to wield the special "big stick" diplomacy and bravado that America needs now more than ever. The present global geopolitical shift has already begun to destabilize parts of the world and is a factor within the present administration and world order.

Trump's flaws are self-defeating and are tied largely to his emotional baggage. He is unable to detach himself from taking everything personally, which signals a high deficiency in empathy and emotional quotient. He wants retribution and revenge against other politicians and government workers for doing their jobs which might not be to his liking or desire. His inability to separate himself and his personality from his political challenges and opponents are a major weakness as a political leader. Without his emotional baggage and his deep desire and need to be narcissistic,

Trump would have established himself as an American stalwart with a great capacity for empathy and undiminished vision. It is no secret that a certain type of mentality, both male and female would want to be attracted to this strong Trumpian mentality and attitude. They see something in Donald Trump that they wish to see in themselves. They are enthralled by his hard-hitting attitude. The strong male alter ego brand that Trump brings to the table is lopsided and found wanting due to the fact, it is not tempered with any substantial measure of empathy or understanding of human nature. We can acknowledge, or understand that God in all His omniscience and omnipotence, wisdom and glory, chose to display attributes other than a divinity wrapped up in an all-male dominated egoistic complex. We should also understand that humans are complex beings, we live a life of futility if we are bugged and burdened by self-absorption.

The rehabilitation effort to save face, refusal to accept his election loss and concede to Joe Biden in good faith is nothing short of total personal weakness. Before the electorate had voted, Trump had already strategized by using his psyches, starting to sing the song of a stolen election, in case he lost. No one could have guessed that Trump was serious to the extent that he would take his stolen election claim to level of insanity many months and years after the election. Many people are still dumbfounded in disbelief that he is stuck in the past. His psychotic claims and tunes are still ringing and still burning in their ears. This is the kind of leadership qualities, influence and role model many Republican identify with and find alluring enough to destroy America, in the name of a half-baked psychopath. It would require an unusual mentality, and a mental process bordering on insanity and lunacy to continue such brazen madness. Some observers claim, the yes men and women parading as Senators, ambushing and defeating the purpose of their office, are still fighting Donald Trump's battle and defending his Big Lie. Their incompetence at managing the Constitution and upholding its sacred statutes is alarming.

This is an indication of how far the country has drifted in

spirit and strength of character. America will be a dark place if it is not rescued by level heads and steady arms.

The leaders of the Republican Party are failing to serve as stewards and gatekeepers of the Constitution and the Democratic process. After 240 years of independence and the taking of Oath by past presidents, it takes one misfit to do the opposite of what he swore to do. This brings into focus the question of trust, accountability, good character and principle. There is value in a man's word and his purpose in office. History testifies, no other president did the opposite of what he had sworn to do. Why go through all this to pussy-foot with American democracy, the Constitution, and the Republican Party? The only alternative to the Democrats, to repair the breach, keep morality in check, to balance internal and external affairs, keep the country from going off the rails, what's the point in all this?

It's all about one man's battered and bruised ego.

All the clamoring about the election being stolen is a face-saving farce and an ego-repair mechanism crap to not appear as a loser. Trump's over-sensitive and unstable nature have overshot its relevance and is now toppling the Republican Party, leaving a stunted group of individuals, whose mindset and mentality has narrowed significantly, stunted group of individuals with little or no understanding of what the Republican Party has stood for or what the GOP is all about. They have totally misconstrued the GOP's purpose.

In comparison, it is much easier to damage the GOP than the Democratic Party. The GOP is like a chaste and refined virgin with spiritual and physical boundaries that are important for maintaining its relevance, purpose and significance. If these qualities are not maintained the party becomes an empty shell. The GOP has ingrained standards, principles, and codes of conduct to guide the party to fulfill its god given purpose to keep and protect American democracy and the constitution.

It is not dictated by a human liberation construct.

Trump's Unbecoming Character

It must be that Trump was overtaken by a moment of weakness or, a lapse of presidential awareness and judgement when he stood to incite the invasion and assault on the Capitol. Was it a scant regard or disrespect for the office he held as chief executive, commander in chief and head of state, in the most powerful nation on earth. This is totally insane. With constitutional guard rails and laws to prohibit such actions, is it possible that a President can put aside his presidential responsibilities, lose his wits, and stand on a platform in front of an armed radical mob to try to overturn an election result? This is beyond imagination, this was broadcast live on all the major US networks for the entire world to witness.

If this is Trump's normal modus operandi, or the sum total of his mental state, then everything else he does is only a pretense and a farce, a make belief, only to gloat in his own capabilities and to camouflage his underlying true nature and mental disarray without regard or concern for laws, boundaries, or principles. It is shameful to put into perspective that in his moment of human weakness and selfish relapse, no one came to the president's rescue to redeem him from his destructive and rebellious narratives, to offer wise counsel or sound judgement on behalf of the executive branch or the Constitution. Nobody defended the democratic ideals on which the American republic stands. They threw it all away in the blink of an eye for the sole purpose of rubbing their cheeks and lips on a mortal's ass.

In 2024, Republicans must ask themselves the question, can Trump lead them to the political promised land, not just to win an election, can he remain stable and deliver? The American people will decide. The Trump presidency started to lose its bearings, character and purpose early in its term. As not to overlook its accomplishments and achievements, His presidency must be credited for increasing middle-class family income, record low unemployment for women, record GDP growth, growth of small business confidence, and greater choices in consumer health care.

Despite the accomplishments under his presidency, Trump, the "ruff cut" and loutish politician cost the GOP and the country dearly, brining into focus more, his negatives than positives. Trump, with His lack of fitness for office and his brand of politics have done irreparable damage to American politics. From a political point of view, you may not see the damage done, depending on the side you are looking from, you may even say that the emperor has on clothes, when we all know the emperor is naked.

Before the Trump presidency, the nation was already divided with more than its share of social and deep racial challenges. Politicians, stakeholders, and religious leaders were cognizant of these challenges. Many attempts were made to reconcile the differences and change the language used. Programs were implemented and crafted to heal the divisions and understand the cultural differences in workplaces. It makes sense, to bridge the gap and alleviate the racial tensions.

Politics was already a dog fight kind of sport, but during Trump's presidency, it was a blood sport. Trump's brand of politics introduced meanness, baseness, open vitriolic discourse, and coarseness to his own party members and the opposition on a level not seen or heard of before. Degeneracy and unkindness have been elevated to levels not before experienced or seen in American politics. It is insane to think about the brutishness that came to light. Members of Congress targeted, bullied, and sent threatening messages. A significant number of Republicans are secretly or openly affiliated to one or more of its numerous right wing white supremacist groups and far right organizations. They display aggressive behavior to members of Congress and anyone who opposes the former president.

Threats made to hurt and to maim, disrespectful name calling became the norm and part of the daily diet in congress. To call to serve is now a fearful endeavor. Trumpism has introduced to American Politics an era of conflict and silent political warfare that America has never seen or experienced before. In effect, Trump opened a rusty can of worms. Members of Congress are targeting each other and normalizing boorishness and crass shameful behavior, extending from Congress to the man in the street.

Trump, his VP pick, J D Vance and allies, paramilitary and army of far-right White Supremacist now complete a triangle that American history has seen and experienced before, this triangle coupled with the Project 2025 agenda will only make matters worse. The second coming of Trump to lead a racially diverse America with his tone of revenge and harsh rhetoric is a powder keg ready to go off.

A president is not expected to overreact or out-do himself. He should be able to rise to the occasion with a calm and clear mental focus. He should be able to envision the end of a situation before it begins, it is called foresight. If he starts to mentally sway or drift from a topic like a tree in a storm, and not clear in his communication and delivery of what was and what should be, instead, start speaking gibberish that inflame, agitate, embitterer or enrage, instead of a wise counsel, giving inspiring and uplifting words, then you will know that his character is terribly flawed.

Bruce Mazlish wrote in the NY Times, dated (Oct. 8, 72) commenting on James Barber's writings in the Book "Presidential Character," Mazlish wrote, "Nobody can doubt that character shapes a president's policy and performance, and that character manifest itself even if darkly and through a mottled mirror." He added, "By establishing these facts firmly, James Barber has established a great deal." What are some of the facts Barber had presented about presidential character?

Barber claims that there are factors that place a person in one of four psycho-political categories,

Patterns in a person's character

These are the factors,
World view
Political style and tone
Power situation
Climate of expectations

These are the psycho-political categories that these factors dictate
Active – positive
Active – negative
Passive – positive
Passive – negative

My interpretation
Active – Positive, a president is positively engaged and hinged
Active – negative, a president is negatively engaged and hinged
Passive – Positive, a president is non engaged and hinged
Passive - Negative a president is non engaging
and unhinged

What are some of Barber's facts regarding a president's character?

We can anticipate a president's behavior and performance by patterns in his
character, world views and political style.
A Presidents behavior is driven by character
A president with self-esteem problems makes terrible leaders.

There is practically nothing that can be done about a president's character when he is already hardened, set, and fully seasoned in his ways. Good or bad, he is going to do what his character dictates without regard for the law, the Constitution, justice, social or political consequences.

James Barber wrote about presidential character and presented some interesting insights to his readers. He claimed that a president's actions, behaviors, and performance can be predicted and anticipated based on the patterns in his character. Therefore, we should not be surprised or alarmed because we already knew and saw it coming, before the actions were manifested.

We already know before we vote what we will get from the former president. The direction of a country boils down to the leader's character. A president can bring democracy to its knees, transform well thinking politicians and law-abiding citizens into rebels, zealots, and terrorists, transform a premium functioning political party and its members into a cult, appealing to the base human nature of hate, fear mongering, rebellion and hostility.

Past Presidents' Quotes about Character
Dwight Eisenhower 1890-1969

The qualities of a great man are vision,
integrity, courage, understanding, the power of
articulation and profundity of character.
—Dwight Eisenhower

Calvin Coolidge 1872-1933

Character is the only secure foundation of the state.
—Calvin Coolidge

Theodore Roosevelt 1858-1919
Americanism is a question of principle, purpose,
of idealism, of character. It is not a matter of
birthplace or creed or line of descent.
—Theodore Roosevelt

Richard Nixon 1913-1994
With all the power that a president has the most
important thing to bear in mind is this: you must not
give power to a man unless above everything else, he has
character. Character is the most important qualification
of the president of the United States can have.
—Richard Nixon

Webster's Quotes on Character
In each human heart are a tiger, a pig, an ass, and a nightingale,
diversity of character is due to their unequal activities.
Ambrose G. Bierce

Truthfulness is a cornerstone in character, and if it be not firmly
Laid in youth, there will ever be a weak spot in the foundation.
—Jefferson Davis

There are no two opinions about the fact that intellect
than riches will lead. It might equally be admitted that
the heart rather than the intellect will eventually lead.
Character, not brain, will count at the crucial moment.
Jefferson Davis

Weakness of character is the only defect which cannot be amended.
Duc F. De La Rochefoucauld

A man's character is the reality of himself. His
reputation is the Opinion others have formed of
him. Character is in him; Reputation is from other
people that is the substance, this is the Shadow.
Henry Beech

Trump's Pernicious Attitude

If the truth be spoken square and clear, Donald Trump has desecrated the office of the presidency, hereby disqualify himself. Even if given a second chance, he has proven that he is incapable of reinventing himself. The least he can do is to recycle himself. He has proven to all, time and again, that he is impotently unable to change his tenor or leadership style. The unsubtle tone of the "we and them" divisiveness, the immature teenage type pleading, "they are after us, they are after you" type coded language and psychological messaging only send the wrong message and develop resentment, fear, animosity and bitterness. Like an aged canine's inability to bring you the ball instead of eating it, calcified in its habits and mentality, it can't learn new tricks. Nothing new will be on the table. Trump will not go away silently into the night because he is a spurned lover will not accept no for an answer.

A common thread runs through "overbearing" male figures is, if they are not "it" there should be no one else. The thought of rejection makes them more dangerous. This is a sure sign of psychosis. Biden and Trump are both facing many personal dilemmas, specifically, age, health and mental acuity Trump's litigations and his personal and political baggage are burning factors.

Trump wants to be commander in chief but he has no intention or interest in leading, he will not be a leader, He wants to prove the point that he is not washed up, to get back at his opponents and convince his base that he alone can lead the Republican Party to victory over the Democrats. He is mentally exhausted, tired and uncommitted, overwhelmed, and disinterested. There is no creative juice left in him. All that will be left of Trump will be an empty shell of an old man swinging heavily at his enemies to take revenge and financially replenish his brand at every opportunity he gets. If he should regain the presidency, he will always be looking back at his 2020 loss to Joe Biden. He is still traumatized and obsessed with his 2020 loss demons. He will send out search and destroy missions to cramp, nullify and obliterate his political enemies. Trump has a burning desire to be revengeful. He said it himself, he wants to be the annihilator, why? This is a type of psychosis and derangement.

How can a person be in politics and not have opponents with opposing views and critics? For Trump, four years is not enough time to take revenge on all the souls that have wronged him. It is in his DNA to get even. Another desire Trump has is to free his Jan. 6 co-conspirators from prison, issue presidential pardons, and remove the negative stigma from the Trump brand. His enemies are not people with a life, careers, and a purpose. They are just shitty things who are out to get him. He will continue to swing his big stick and hammer in every direction at individuals, the radical left and fake news. He will continue to manufacture names and belittle his opponents like the school yard bully. Like Don Quixote, he will saddle up every morning and chase the windmills in his head. He will seek to change the laws of the land, make every attempt to influence the Judicial system and launch project 2025. Trump will seek to amend the laws to suit himself and his political and businesses affiliates. He will extend his time in office or install a successor to continue policies behind the scenes.

Trump wants to prove that he is not a one term president. A second term is the gold standard of presidential success. A second time around connotates staying power and not being washed up

It is the cherry on top and the gold ring in presidential talk and circles. It is like being inducted into the hall of fame. Without it, you are not part of the elites, just a one-term president.

Trump is battle worn, a weary soldier with many defeats and losses under his belt, he will continue to leak the soul of the GOP, it's the same alter ego spirit of many failed men who have traversed the public domain as politicians, leaders and kings. As they age and their influence wanes they become stubborn and unyielding. They are not discerning and cannot accept that we are all mere mortals with limited days, forgetting the fact that we all "rust," wear out, get old, weak and tired.

Trump needs a savior. He is backed into a corner, the countless litigations, court rulings, legal cost and fees are like a high mountain to climb in his declining years. He sees the Presidency as his savior and a hiding place. To plug the leak of the soul of the GOP to the Democrats, another Republican nominee must rise up, we all see and understand by now that Trump and Trumpism is a bitter medicine that does little or no good. Otherwise, we will have another four years of the Democrats and the liberal left.

The Republicans and the MAGA cult are willing to make that bet on Trump. Trump winning the Presidency is the least of their worries. Unless he is able to offer a better alternative than Biden and the Democrats to improve their lives, that of their children and grandchildren, to make America truly great again, their valued votes, time and efforts to elevate him a second time to the White House and the pinnacle of American power would be a colossal waste.

Trumpism and the Evangelicals

For many people, Trump's misrepresentation of the 2020 political events is still much more than a lying shame. Too few stood up against the deafening silence, amid vile threats, intimidation, and political banishment from their own party. The silence does more to discredit Evangelicals who have chosen to engage in a politics of convenience, thereby branding themselves more of a political arm of the GOP than an authoritative Christian movement. Evangelicals betrayed their Christian faith for the fickle and capricious Trump. Everyone is entitled to their opinion and political beliefs and persuasion,

As Christians, we are called upon to pray for our leaders, to trust divine providence and wisdom, not to prostrate ourselves physically, mentally or give undeserved glory, honor and praise to a political leader. God always reminds us, "I the Lord thy God am a jealous God," (Deut. 5:9)

Although not as abrasive and as militant as the Proud Boys or as rooted in hatred and racism as white supremacists, Evangelicals are as active, vibrant politically, and are punctuated with diehard Trump activist pastors and church leaders. Under the guise of Christian idealism, many are more zealous in their defense of Trump and his return to the White House than some of their non-Christian political counterparts.

How could this prime Christian body be so deceived? They

sacrificed the faith and honor of Christ for political dregs and religious stain. Could it be that evangelicals chose to fill a void created by Trumpism for the lack of a clear and meaningful agenda or policy, be so willfully blinded, they are convinced that Trump with all his heavy baggage, and skeletons, was God's gift to the American people and the world, so much so that they would rather have rather sell their souls to Trump than to stand up for the rule of law, truth, honesty, principles, and integrity.

Evangelicals knew what they were getting themselves into when they opened themselves up to the sleaze, smut and smudginess of Trump and Trumpism. Evangelicals would not admit, in their moment of indiscretion and spiritual blindness, they were caught up in the euphoria of Trumpism and the hype of personality politics that had engulfed the MAGA movement. They chose to remain silent and quietly invigorate, rather than repudiate Trump and his lying schemes while he assaults truth, the rule of law, the Constitution, and the American government.

No attempt was made by Evangelicals to admonish or remind supporters, law makers and the former President, of the high value of truthfulness, honesty fairness and integrity of character as it relates to Christian beliefs and conduct. We all witnessed the growth of Trump's fanatic supports, How they Morphed into the MAGA cult, an unpredictable uncontrollable political untamed movement, disregarding civil norms and Constitutional boundaries. Many Evangelical pastors would disagree, but the real proof is in their action and inaction which speak louder than their words. They would pray, beg and plead with God to put new wine and a new brain in Trump's "old wineskin." (Mark 2: 22) Despite their fervent prayers, and the laying of hands, on Trump, the political Christian apostles never seek wise counsel or persistently knock on doors for truth, honestly and integrity. Their unified voice was their defense of Trump, not the truth, unty of purpose and the Constitution. They did not petition for Godly wisdom and insights, they only saw what they wanted to see and heard what they wanted to hear.

In the history of American politics, Evangelicals have never been so visibly loud and politically active than during the Trump presidency. It is quite obvious, comparatively, the political leader with the most decrepit character, the swiftest of lips, the craftiest of fingers, and the most lying tongue, who willfully distorts the truth and knowingly misinforms, he is mounted on a decorated pedestal and gets all the praise and adoration from today's spiritually dehydrated Evangelicals. It is also ironic that this expert and wizard in dishing out sleazy names is perceived by Evangelicals as messianic, therefore, in their spiritually blinded eyes he can do no wrong. To many in the Evangelical circle, the coming of the "merchant of chaos" is more anticipated than the Second Coming of the true Messiah. It's no wonder he is confounded, bounded, and buried under an avalanche of controversies, litigation, and accusations, evangelicals can't see this because in their eyes, Trump is a God send. 2024 will be the make-or-break moment for Trump, the crowning of the "MAGA king," or the sink to rise no more dilemma. Will Evangelicals continue to allow themselves to be tarnished or will they see the signs and drift away. It is all to be seen in the 2024 presidential election spectacle.

It is difficult to comprehend the marriage between Trump and Evangelicals Christians. Is it an innocent patriotic relationship or is there more to it than what meets the eyes? Is there an undermining, an ungodly under current driving Evangelicals to belittle, disparage, and malign the Christian faith in exchange for the MAGA hype, also, to associate Bible thumping congregants with QAnon mass, to dilute the Gospel, confuse and disorient Christians experiencing the new birth in Christ and those who want to make a full commitment to the Gospel of Christ?

There is strong evidence, by their words and fanatical actions, there is an unholy alliance between Trump and Evangelicals. Why else would a prominent Christian group endorse and be an ally with a narcissistic, self-absorbed mortal who shows scant regard for Christian values. The display of evangelical pastors prostrating sanctified domains in the name of Trump on national TV and worldwide audiences is sacrilegious. It is not possible for Trump and this Christian group to consort themselves without stretching their necks to indulge and partake from the pasture of Donald Trump

There is likely some sort of agreement or compromise for political milage. Based on their own biases, Evangelicals believe what they want to believe and construe the Bible and their faith any which way they choose to satisfy their beliefs. Part of that belief system is that Trump needed them, (Evangelicals) and they needed Trump, they believe, God cannot be found beyond their purview, therefore Trump is the only vessel of clay that God can use.

The assumption in some quarters is that Trump is a wolf in sheep's clothing, a person who resorts to using Christian and religious parlance and jargon, taking Bible picture props, making religious appeals, appearing in Evangelical circles to convince others and to appear as an angel of light. For these and other ill- advised reasons they choose to accommodate his glaring indiscretions, misconduct, and character faults. They hear no evil, see no evil and speak no evil of Trump. To break down the psychology and dissect the mentality of this strange union is one that begs the question, is this a union with God's approval, or are Evangelicals being deceived by Satan? This is an important and significant phenomenon, spiritually and politically, this has never happened in the history of American politics, a character of disrepute, elevated, approved and endorsed by a major Christian organization.

Evangelicals and other Christian organizations are important branches of American spiritual and religious life, they are called by God to spread the Gospel of Christ and to win dying souls in preparation for eternal life. Therefore, they cannot defraud or shortchange themselves, their faith and Christian values because of this grave and solemn responsibility that has been entrusted to them.

Evangelicals are called out by God with a mandate of faith for eternal life. They are the gatekeepers and stewards of human life and earth's experience, entrusted with a sacred responsibility as administrators and agents of the Gospel of Christ, not to unashamedly display evidence of spiritual radicalization or exhibit signs of moral collapse by blindly attaching themselves to a political character and a cultish group. This spiritual and political compromise of the evangelical right attaching themselves unconditionally to a character of disrepute undoubtedly casts a shadow on the power of the Gospel to seek and save lost souls at any cost.

Evangelicals, once a bold and effective, "stand between," heaven and hell for wayward souls, seeking redemption, direction and spiritual guidance, now bow their heads in continuous silence in the Malaise and decrepitude of Donald Trump. The salt of the earth seems to have lost its Savor.

The Argument,
Evangelical Response to
Mr. Worldly Wise

Trump's magnetic pull was too strong for many to resist, especially for white Evangelicals. They respond very favorably to his beck and call, psychological wizardry, charisma, and magic. Trump is much too profound and sophisticated for the typical Bible Belt white Evangelicals and the lighthearted evangelical Christians who are merely church goers with no spiritual depth. They are gullible and can be easily beguiled by a white Republican Male who is, a wealthy businessman, his photogenic social media family completes his personal and family profile, the trappings are all there, very hard to resist.

With Donald Trump, white Evangelicals don't know, they fail to understand that there are many layers, and deep levels to Trump, as a person of interest. The master financial craftsman and worldly-wise Don worships at the altar of the God of Mammon. Therefore, in everything he does, money is the common denominator. It comes first and last, his main objective, overriding everything else, money is the dominant motivating factor in everything he does. Secondly, with his obsessive self-absorption and over-indulgence in his persona and personal accomplishments of me, myself, I alone can fix it, there is little or no space for anyone else to take center stage.

The evangelical-Trumpian mix is more than politics, it brings into focus the term, "cult," the word associates with, or means, misplaced or excessive admiration of a particular person or leader, hence the term "personality cult." Trump, the egomaniac self-worshiper and Evangelicals, the question is, how do these two opposite poles on every spectrum, morality, ethics, truth and human relationship, selflessness and benevolence find a compromise to the point that they are tightly entwined, so as to bond themselves in a deadly embrace to turn a blind eye to the basic truths of the Bible and the sacred teachings of the Christan faith, to the extent that nothing else seems to matter, creating a moral and spiritual vacuum from the White House to church pews.

Evangelical's Argument and Response

"We have a right to choose in the best interests of a country founded on biblical principles. We see Mr. Trump as a God send, some of us to the point of idolizing him. We agree, Trump has his flaws and faults, as we all do, nevertheless, we stand with Trump and all his baggage."

Mr. Worldly Wise's argument and response.

"As Christian conservatives, do you understand that he is a divisive secularist? You are giving cover and approval to a daringly offensive character who cares next to nothing about others or their point of view. If you don't bow to him or share his opinions, you are the worst of the worst. Do you think that others who are not of the faith, including non-believers, who are spiritually weak and are not spiritually attached, witnessing this unfaltering loyalty, encouraged by the torch bearers of the Christian faith, joining the chorus of personality cult, instead of avoiding political mudslinging and moral morass. It's now clearly seen that Trumpism has devoured and hollowed out Christian conservatives so much so that their independent cognitive ability has been obliterated."

Evangelical's argument and response.

"Mr. Worldly Wise, understand this, we view the world through the eyes of God and the Bible, many say Mr. Trump is a broken and warped vessel. He might be broken but God is the Potter, He specializes and can mend any broken vessel including Trump. In a time as this, we need someone with the boldness of Trump to stand up to the leftist agenda. We as Evangelicals strive and aspire to obey God's words and adhere to his principles."

In the not too-distant past, the Bible, prayers, and Christian values were integral parts of American lives, the society and its school system. Look closely at what is happening to our society, Families, homes, and school are being overtaken and torn apart by the demons of depression, drugs, suicide, and murder. Left activist made a conscious decision to exclude and erase God's Words and His presence from American lives consciousness, classrooms, schools and families.

As Evangelicals we aspire for an American society where the Word of God and his precepts are appreciated and respected. God's precepts should take precedent over everything else. Mr. Trump is a broken man yes, but we know what is in his heart. He will not take us further left to the point of no return."

Mr. Worldly Wise's argument and response

"Sorry to disappoint or burst your bubble Evangelicals, just in case you have been sleeping and have been unaware, Mr. Trump does not have the storage capacity, bandwidth or character for what it takes to be the next president. He might have been great in his first attempt to "make America great again." Now that we have seen and experienced what he is all about, it was not a beautiful sight. It was a very rocky road. At this pivotal juncture in American history, he has proven time and again that he does not have the calling or the intestinal fortitude to begin the social and mental fine tuning necessary to move America forward. He is both crass and course, too vindictive of a character to initiate the national upliftment we all crave. He is not a good example for positive impressions or a source of inspiration for old or young impressionable minds.

Your salient points are taken and noted carefully, but you are barking up the wrong tree. Trump can't take us there, he is lost in a maze of contempt, egotism and self-absorption. Correct you are, the United States as a nation has been backsliding for decades and needs spiritual injection, moral renewal and regeneration. The signs and red flags are there, he will only take us back in time and into the dark ages"

Opening a Can of Worms
(2008 and 2012 election Flashback and review)

After Barack Obama won the 2008 election, the assessments and reviews were critical, harsh, and discerning. Energy, effort and valuable time were invested in finding solutions and answers to the continuous dismal showing of the GOP at the polls. Since the 2008 election, there have been endless lists, analytical reports and reviews. In 2012, having lost the popular vote in the last six presidential elections, the Republican Party was ready and prepared to self-evaluate and present a comprehensive evaluation, which came in the form of a report called the "Growth and Opportunity Project." It was also called the "GOP Autopsy Report." The purpose of this report was to trouble-shoot the losses, repair the damage, and devise a blueprint to move forward as a strong and viable alternative to the Democrats.

The GOP autopsy report, along with other reviews, recommended that the GOP be more flexible and be rebranded as a kinder and more inclusive GOP with a softer tone and broader outreach, as opposed to the idea that "Republicans don't care." It was argued that the party had to return to its roots, accepting and engaging the principles and fundamentals that had propelled the GOP as symbolic of family, trust, hard work, and Christian values. It was about fiscal conservatives and patriotic Americans. It was further argued that although the GOP had lost focus, the essential themes of fiscally responsible, low on taxes were essential themes.

Calls were made for the party to reconcile its agenda on the role of government and to include a policy on economic growth through taxation and fiscal restraint. It was further recommended that a "Reaganite" be found to unite the party and reach out to women and minorities. The autopsy report bemoaned the fact that the GOP was continuously marginalizing itself and instead should be more welcoming, and that the concerns and plight of women should not be taken lightly but highlighted and addressed.

Having these important features, recommendations, and objectives implemented would rebrand the GOP as a viable and strong alternative to the Democrats. After months of hard work, gathering the data, reviews, reports, recommendations and evaluations, the party is now in the red facing double and triple jeopardy, all more like a pipe dream coming down a golden escalator to be thrown out the window.

1. The GOP's autopsy report and recommendations were totally ignored.
2. The Republicans Party with Trump as the head cook is brewing a pot of retribution mixed with revenge, moving the party in the opposite direction.
3. Republicans are once again on the back foot running another losing race, making a mockery of the predecessors, effectively causing them to turn like spindles in their graves.

Both Trump and the GOP had no impulsion to take the party in dire straits that the party now finds itself, it's more a matter of both Trump and his base surviving off each other's energy symbiotically. Trump looked to his base to be fed with their approval and loyalty, and the base looked to Trump for its preservation, sense of belonging and entitlement in a changing political dynamic.

The Trump's Ecosystem
and a Can of Worms

A new era of American politics began with the presidency of Donald Trump. In a matter of months, the GOP reversed its trend from a principled, moralistic, and decorous organization, a vibrant, clear running refreshing stream to a stagnant pond. As other literary observers have described the GOP "a morally repellant GOP," now named the "Grumpy Old Party." Documented actions displayed by senators, party leaders and party members testify to the accuracy of these statements. Trump projecting the Big Lie as a political platform and a major political talking point, took the GOP by storm, and they did not hesitate to run with this false and misleading message. For four years it was being peddled as the main gripe of Donald Trump. How is it possible that the GOP did not see where Trump in his limited perception was taking them with his betrayal of his constitutional responsibilities as a former President. His careless and irresponsible actions bear witness to the shallowness, the grounding mental state of leaders within the GOP's hierarchy. The question is, why were they willing to sacrifice the GOP and their consciences for Donald Trump's crap, was it worth it?

In this the twenty-first century, the GOP has regressed significantly, and it can only find its footing by nominating a true thoroughbred Republican candidate. Since Donald Trump took office, the GOP has been in a whirlwind, experiencing a wild "topsy-turvy" ride. No one in the GOP wants to bell the cat or admit juvenile delinquency in the actions and the devolution of the GOP under the leadership of the former President or have him accountable for his actions. They have already made up their minds to be washed away with Trump's ever flowing river of shenanigans.

The Trump-initiated GOP's backsliding became quite evident in real time. A significant section of the Republican base, including lawmakers, senators, and party leaders, have chosen to generate and prorogate a theme of conflict in word and deeds. This include threats, retribution, political ambushes and personal attacks. You ask yourself the question, "is this possible, is this a reality, in today's modern democratic American society and politics?"

Up until the Trump presidency, the legacy of the GOP could be described as glowing. The critical and important issues to be addressed were being attended to. The party knew what it was about, its ideals and principles, values were adhered to, its ideology was intact. Party leaders and the GOP base knew what they had to do to win an election, and what they had to do to take the party forward, as documented in the GOP's growth and opportunity project and the 2008 autopsy reports. Then came President Donald Trump. The bile injected vindictiveness and stubborn political soreness has its origin in the mentality and psyche of Mr. Trump. His unwillingness to rise above himself in the strength of a man with human forthrightness, to look truth, justice and veracity in the eye is nothing short of personal weakness.

It is quite clear that the former president was willing to put American democracy on the line to satisfy his fragile ego. We are all humans, and we understand each other's motives, mentalities and intentions, we all knew and could tell that Trump was severely wounded psychologically, mentally and emotionally by the loss of the 2020 election. His ego took a devastating blow at the loss and he continues to deny the 2020 Election result. Those who continue to support his false claim help him perpetuate his demented actions and sink further into a state of deranged irrationality. In any combat situation, blows are given and received. There will be a winner and a loser, both parties cannot win. His actions depict a huge measure of psychosis and irresponsible conduct.

If Trump was more traditional, knowledgeable and informed about the history of the Americas, particularly the United States, and appreciative of the sacrifices that were made by the founding fathers. The men and women who served, fought, bled, and died for independence, liberty, freedom, dignity and civil rights. They paid the price and the consequences and repercussions in their lives and bodies. Had the former president been equipped with the knowledge of the fact, that the blood, sweat and tears of broken bodies and spirits were shed to achieve the basic human and civil rights and, to secure and preserve American lives and values, free speech, justice for all and the pursuit of happiness and a democratic union. Armed with this knowledge and respect of the fallen, he would not have trampled the Constitution and the hard-earned democratic process. If he was endowed with the understanding of the gravity and the character that presidential awareness demands, he would have foreseen and discerned the imprudence and lunacy of his actions, in leading the nation down a rugged path. The GOP leaders were afraid to speak truth to power, and be rational, preferring not to rattle themselves and others to defend Trump's nefarious action, pouring "salt" into the psycho-social wounds, pain and fears of the marginalized and minorities. On top of all these challenges, Trump chose to open a can of worms, added anxiety and toxicity to the social fabric.

Before he took office in 2016, no one knew what to expect of the businessman, former TV host and entertainer. No one could have predicted under his presidency the GOP would have lost its innocence and go so rogue. Several factors that propel the roguery and sent the GOP into a spiraling smog are;

1. the tone and influence of Trump's course and crude character

2. the gullibility of the Republican base not Trump's falsehood and lying schemes
3. the anti-social and paramilitary groups that permeate the GOP.

In this type of GOP's "cult-blurred" environment, Trump get the opportunity to flourish in his element and display his true colors. He can speak absurdities and tickle their funny bones, since they are convinced that he is funny and smart. Never in a hundred years would anyone believe that there would be legislators, Senators and Governors willing to legislate and suppress the vote and voice of Americans. Revise and initiate the Gerry Mandarin Code, devise ways to make it more difficult for their fellow Americans to exercise their right to vote. This is one of the many spin-offs of the Big Lie, a component and ingredient of the can of worms that the former president chose to open. The can of worms Trump opened began with the Big Lie, members of his party were glad to digest and run with it. These worms take the forms of pugnacious, antagonistic, and repressive actions, which seem to be some form of GOP retribution and MAGA appeasement for Trump's failure to secure the votes to win the 2020 election. These "wormy" actions are mostly political vendettas that will continue to be felt and have no social, economic, or moral value or purpose. They intimidate and antagonize the innocent and the electorate. They are crafted after the tone and mentality of Trump. These "wormy" ideas and attitudes keep popping up as they please with an aim and objective to facilitate a political agenda. Trump and the GOP, in a symbolic dance of ill will and meanness, made many attempts to suppress the vote and turn back the hands of time instead of formulating constructive political, social, and economic solutions to make meaningful changes in the lives of Americans.

Before Trump, the waters were not troubled, vitriolic and inflamed sentiments were unheard of in political circles. Politicians respected each other's integrity, sincerity, and veneration as a matter of political principle, respect and comportment. The term, "a can of worms," interpreted to mean, "creating a problematic or complicated situation leading to more problems and complications," became quite evident and a systematic part of the MAGA movement after the 2020 election loss. Blatant lies, distractions, and excuses were employed to prevent a meaningful transition to the Biden Presidency and keep the Republican base distracted and muddled from the real issues affecting the party. What should Trump do to keep himself busy and viable, and stay relevant? A king without a throne or power is like a fish out of water. Other former presidents got themselves occupied meaningfully instead of banging their heads against the wall or kick pricks.

Many poor souls experienced the dark era of the Nazis in Germany and the pain of racism in the segregated South, the misery of man inhumanity to their fellowman. Our distinguished forefathers and visionary leaders drafted a constitution to establish states that were united with a common goal of freedom from inequality and injustice. A union which esteems the Constitution and the underlying principles on which it stands, to help establish democracy in the United States.

Today, it seems like there is a "bogey-man" around every corner, down the stairs and in the basement. Mickey Mouse and Donald Duck can't sleep at night because they are worried about being censored. Disney land in Florda is about to be confiscated after providing thousands of job opportunities, operating as a successful tourist attraction for more than one hundred years. Books, the elite instrument for learning, seem to be losing their prime position. Reading for learning, fun and pleasure might be a thing of the past, they want many to believe creeps are hiding between the pages. Many books are targeted to be banned and delisted from school curriculum in some states and school districts. Many teachers are packing, leaving the classroom in droves, they can't teach what their school curriculum dictates, they have to teach a political agenda in some subject areas. The theory of race (Critical Race Theory, CRT) and its academic connotations and significance is also on the Republican's cut and repair chopping block of listed item that should be stripped from academic influence. The major concern about Critical Race Theory is its perceived economic social, and political influence, as with other issues will it add or subtract from political clout.

In June 2022, the Supreme Court overturned the 1973 Roe v Wade ruling left women with little or no choice about their own bodies, even in the face of physical, mental abuse, rape and death. The 2022 ruling gives few options as it pertains to factors affecting women's gynecological needs, mental health and well-being.

The Trump era seem to have introduced the advancement of the judiciary and the executive branches of government in partnership rather than being independent branches, giving off a strong whiff of judicial activism and activist courts, were justices turned their faces to a political ideology and agenda and their backs on justice free of political interference, created more complications and problematic outcomes.

"Wokeness," which is a private personal mental construct, which we all have, is now looked at as a barefooted criminal being hounded by self-appointed culture warriors. Being "woke,"- an affirming mental state, is now a political issue, and a political problem, flagged as a menace and a misdemeanor by reason of "wokeness."

Untangling Trumpism and the GOP

The schemes of bitterness, malice, ripe animosity and deep-seated revenge are the embarrassing reactions to the loss at the 2020 election. This was born from a character with no regard for statutes or laws, the caustic remarks and reactions are to satisfy personal psychological defects that many people would rather ignore than to face the truth. What else could have driven a person to exhibit such repulsive abnormal behavior to a pass event such as an election loss? It is a done deal, and even the dead would have seen and acknowledged the results as settled dust. Led by the psychologically impaired and wounded choir master, Trump himself, some people would rather dim their wits than to be honest with themselves.

The proponents of the Big Lie were hoping to pull off the big election scam by sticking to their guns that the election was stolen. They were hoping to get lucky by hanging their hopes and political futures on Donald Trump's star power. Some thought they might get lucky, but many did not. The midterm election and the anticipated "Red Wave" told a different story, it failed to become a reality, many people were not buying the Big Lie. The investments they had in Trump's false claim did not materialize as expected.

The courts ruled that the half-baked litigations brought to nullify and void election results in some states were unfounded, after ballot counts and recounts by the courts, "there is no proven case of outright election fraud, simply being interpreted, the cry of "wolf wolf," the Big Lie of an election fraud was nothing more than a cheap political scam. It is almost incomprehensible that in today's postmodern America, a political scam like the Big Lie was allowed to take root, flourish and grow to the extent that it did, to prop up a major political party and be a platform to launch a political comeback. The big question is now being asked, "is running against the truth and the United States Constitution a winning strategy for the 2024 election campaign? Can lies and premeditated false assumptions in a political or spiritual context outlast truth and fairness?

The human spirit is a discerner of truth and character. It enlightens us all to a greater good, responding independently of our own biases, wills and desires. You can fool some of the people, some of the time, but you can't fool all the people all the time. The United States is a boiling pot of emotion and racism, conspiracy theorists and professional talking heads, promoting divisiveness, lies, and hate. Despite this, truth, goodness and fairness will rise above all the impurities of the human soul.

The Big Lie is an insult to intelligence and the Constitution. It is a savage attack that threatens the rule of law and order in a civilized society. It is juvenile in its conception, awkward, crocked and lopsided. It is appalling that the brains and minds in so called high places, the leadership of the GOP willfully close their eyes, went to sleep, chose to sell themselves and play along in a clown's circus of self-deceit. They have proven themselves guilty and have betrayed their country. The summary of Trump's minions and their defense of the election lie is nothing but a showboating circus, GOP's politicians and some GOP party members on talk shows, podcast, interviews, all appear and sound cynical, full of snicker, insincere and misleading.

The United States Constitution cannot be penetrated or manipulated by lazy minds or cheap shots taken by losing politicians. It is a charter of constituted statutes. An essential fact is that order rules the universe in every spiritual, divine and physical sense. If chaos, disorder, lawlessness and anarchy prevail, or get in the social clockwork by destroying unity and consensus, the scope and purpose of the "Union" the pursuit of happiness, the American Dream will crumble or collapse. The Constitution was formulated out of the objective and aspiration of like-minded men of principle, honesty and virtue, inspired by Godly wisdom and vison, befitting of a God blessed republic immune to autocrats, overlords and tyrants. It is very discomforting, the pain and chaos that Trumpism and the "Trump-pets" have unleashed, a barrage of negative actions and attitudes to everything normal, democratic and constitutional.

The former president and his defenders have become enlightened culture warriors, these Trump defenders are always prepared and ready to mother and defend Trump and his unconstitutional and unlawful activities, to embolden and invigorate the GOP base.

With the Constitution being pressured, attacked and abused, weakened and watered down to the level of liars, unprincipled and unethical individuals, what will be left of the republic will be dregs at the bottom of the barrel. The continuous pussy footing with the sacred Constitution will eventually cause it to lose its purpose and validity. For this reason, the GOP must entangle itself from Trumpism.

Although Trumpism runs deep and wide in the Republican Party, the GOP must rediscover its roots and equip itself for the 2024 election. The 2024 presidential election win or lose is of paramount importance. There is much invalidating opinion on Trumpism, it cannot be described as an ideology, because of its lack of defined principles, rules and goals. Its ambiguity, fanaticism and personality worship make it more easily defined as a glorified cult.

Another problem with Trumpism is its negative tones of animosity, retribution, bigotry and racism which rings much louder than its policies. The GOP cannot thrive in such a political and socially acidic environment, this kind of sourness is not conducive to its own growth and relevance as a major political party. Spinelessness is the order of the day. Under Trumpism, no one has an opinion or point of view, if they do, they have to keep their opinions to themselves, in "Trump land" no one wants to stand on their own two feet.

Trump thinks he alone defines, interprets, understands, and says it all. According to Donald, no one else can do, or knows it better than he does. If he is going over the edge or in a pit, its "cluck, cluck, cluck," his loyal fans are behind him like chickens without heads, if he says he is a Dragon that breathes fire they believe him, if he says come let's invade the Capitol and have an insurrection, without a second thought his loyal party members are ready, this is contrary to human rationality. Therefore, for its own sustainability and betterment, the GOP must extricate and disentangle itself from the weight and harmful deposits of the "Trump culture."

The Trump culture breeds authoritarianism, which is the repression of free thought, removal of individual freedom, opinions, actions, and choices. Another facet of Trumpism is Nationalism, which excludes other nationalities, a country standing by itself, in spite of all odds. Its foreign policy excludes allies, international partnerships and consensus. Trumpism brings divisive rhetoric and blatant disregard for democratic and electoral norms, skeptical of government control and disregard for existing laws.

Trumpism, stripped to its core, is a very flammable political culture that pours scorn on democracy and is not in favor of existing democratic norms, processes or existing laws. Outsiders and immigrants are not welcomed because they are derivatives of "shit-hole countries." They are immigrant invaders coming to steal our jobs on farms and in hospitals. They take away cleaning jobs from American workers.

Since the cult of personality politics have overtaken the GOP, some of its core principles and Republican ideology have been silently pushed out the back door to make way for the Trump doctrine, which present a stark contrast and permanent impairment of the GOP. If Trump wins the presidency, he will place the Republican Party in a serious predicament. He has not proven himself worthy of the faith, confidence, and loyalty that members of the GOP have invested in him. He will continue to trample and squander their trust and belief in him with disappointments, blunders, miscalculations, and inefficiency. Trump will do further damage to the Republican Party by changing the cultural ethos of the party. He will indulge in pettiness, trivialities, and triflings over policy, substance, and performance.

The GOP has sold its God-given birthright to the Democrats. The embrace of Trump by the Republican Party is a fleeting dance of convenience that will leave the GOP high and dry with little opportunity for future growth and progress. It will backslide the Republican Party to 2008 and 2013. After great losses to the Democrats, there was a reckoning and a wake-up call to recalibrate and resuscitate the GOP, resulting in the 2013 autopsy report. The GOP has become an empty dream without an ideology, direction, a policy, an agenda or a political platform. The Republican Party's birthright to leadership must be reclaimed by untangling the GOP from the Trump syndicate.

Trump's Purpose and Spiritual Significance

Donald Trump's rise to leader of the GOP has been extraordinary. Trump's ability to prevail over all odds is supernatural. Several factors have caused a majority of the Republican base to turn away from the Republican Party and embrace Trump. The Republican Party has been dismantled and is in disarray, it lacks vision, direction and an identity. Trump is not the leader of the Republican Party; he is the leader of his own club. This wing of the Republican Party, awakened and energized by Trump, has enough political clout to do whatever they want to do. It will become more damaging if Mr. Trump reclaims the presidency.

We all know what is in the heart and mind of Trump. It is no secret. He is outspoken and does not hold his cards close to his chest. He speaks his mind. Trump and his base are far removed from the realities and seriousness of the times. This is not a proud dance; it is a wounded limp. Trump is fighting unending allegations, indictments, and fines. He is a wounded and frustrated human being. Some of the politicians who once disparaged him have turned around and are propping him up and fighting his many battles. Lifting the country economically, socially, politically, internationally, and intellectually will be a daunting task. Nobody knows how he will interact with those who have challenged him. Nobody knows how he will interact with those who have different points of view, a clear vision, a sense of purpose, know-how and intelligence.

The inability to displace Trump from his political perch proves that he has a spiritual mandate and an end-time purpose in the scheme of things to come. His political dominance and influence will not be terminated until his purpose has been realized and fulfilled. This will be revealed during the 2024 presidential election. Trump returning to the White House is still a great possibility. Whether or not Trump is successful in his presidential bid, he has already done the damage and fulfilled his mandate.

Trump influenced the world for four years and will continue to play a part in social and political development. He is setting the stage for racial and political tension to explode. This is in preparation for the end-time convergence of humankind. It is the continuous spiritual conflict of evil versus good and Jesus Christ versus Lucifer. It will bring a new heaven and a new earth, ultimately bringing an end to our earthly dispensation. This has nothing to do with the interpretation that Trump is evil and Democrats are good, or that Trump is the Devil and will be overtaken by good. Trump is an end-time messenger and a piece of the Biblical puzzle. He is a pawn that is being used to harden and embitter the social and political landscape. This conflict has been in effect since time began. We are all experiencing the unfolding of a predestined schedule.

We are also seeing the rise of artificial intelligence, the impact of climate change, and the continued effects of COVID and other superbugs. American political norms were unshakable for more than two hundred years. Trump's whistles, coded language, and cheap psychology keep pushing their panic buttons on a regular basis. His attitude will upend the social balance and give way to suspicion, distrust, fear, and hatred.

Trump's main purpose it seems, is to irritate and disrupt the political order while hijacking the GOP. Though electable, he is not as "winnable" as some might believe. Donald Trump might retake the presidency and the White House, many in the GOP and the general electorate want to send Trump packing, but they can't. He is like an albatross around the neck of the GOP. Their only option is to endure Donald Trump.

What is the result of making America great? We hear little about agendas, policies, social, economic, and structural plans. There are more conflicts, retribution talk, political infighting than intellectual discourse, problem solving addressing substantive issues affecting the impoverished and the middle class. It is understandable, GOP Politicians favor Trump over the rule of law, making a mockery of the Constitution and the justice system, but not at the expense of making America less great than it already is.

A failed insurrection was historic for any president, but there were also multiple indictments and impeachments. Is it normal for a political leader to be mostly on the wrong side of the law and maintain a leading position in the polls? Trump's mental state and fitness for office have been questioned. He was ridiculed by actors, cartoonist, branded "Orange Jesus." Multiple convictions, both civil and criminal violations, countless attempts have been made on both the left and right to stifle and demolish his political rise and resurgence. All have failed to inflict harm to Trump and slow his dominance of the GOP.

Donald Trump's influence and control of the GOP is compelling, historic, and unprecedented. Never again will another American have a greater impact on a political party than Donald Trump. Trump has tapped into the secret source of the Republican base, and he uses this energy to his advantage, financially and politically. He does and says as he pleases, against his own party members and the opposition. Trump overwhelms his political opponents to remain at the top of the presidential ticket and control political discourse - without any fear of negative consequences or backlash. He has a spiritual mandate to accomplish. Although Trump has been bedeviled by damning reports from psychologists his political opponents, both Democrats and Republicans, his spiritual mandate remains intact and will be accomplished. The assassin's bullet could not stop or reverse this spiritual mandate.

It is evident, since Trump's accent to presidential office, political, social and judicial norms have been broken. The time has come and is ripe to usher in political and social disorder as the end-times demand. The turning point is now, and the rationale is Trump. The racial divide and toxicity have multiplied, there is much hate and anger in society, in the media, at sporting events, on the road, in schools and in Congress. Sanity, fair play, truth, kindheartedness, human understanding, and benevolence are placed on the back burner. Humans hate other humans for their physical features, skin color, accent, place of birth. The social acidity in the American atmosphere is sometimes unbearable.

The political tension will inflict catastrophic damage to the American social structure. The rest of the world will strain under similar challenges. There will be irreversible changes in politics, technology, health care, and climate. These are fundamental threats to human survival.

Where Does Ron DeSantis Fits In?

It's difficult to tell where DeSantis fits in. The much-hyped GOP nonstarter outplayed himself. The rising star was the GOP's heir apparent, but he fizzled like a soda pop. DeSantis fell from the good graces of the media and other social groups. Once the GOP's "darling," he fell to earth, not even with roll a little and endurance. Despite his impressively strong start, DeSantis fell with a flat "dud sound" and stayed fallen. He went from Trump's strongest challenger to Trump's weakest rival.

What if DeSantis had maintained his composure and defied the impulse to combat the woke demons in his mind and the need to preach to the GOP choir? If DeSantis had resisted these urges, his 2024 presidential run would have been his rock star moment. DeSantis was my guy. He was my pick as a suitable alternative to Trump. He was an up-and-coming qualified, genuine Republican candidate for president, clearheaded, motivated, and suave.

During the COVID pandemic, he held his own against all odds. In my estimation, he mostly got lucky. Even though Floridians died by the thousands, DeSantis railed against vaccination. Like everywhere else, Florida was shut down and suffered great loss of life due to COVID. No miracles, magic, or heroic feats were done. Some governors were fortunate to come out on the other side of the pandemic looking better than others, depending on the politics of the virus and its economic impact on the state. Ron DeSantis was one of those lucky governors. COVID was a "work of nature." DeSantis claimed victory over something we have no control over.

As his popularity rose because of the politics of COVID, he started to lose his individuality. He unsuccessfully tried to be a Trump clone and a culture warrior to augment his profile among the Trump-controlled GOP base. This was like placing himself between a rock and a hard place or the devil and the deep blue sea. His political campaign was fighting culture wars, he was not privy to the fact that no one can function effectively as a Trump clone. The Trump psyche is to "sand across the grain." It works well for Trump, not for anyone else. Many people were imploring the Florida Governor to run. "Run Ron Run" they saw in him something special, fresh youthful energy and enthusiasm, his reply, "Just chill," seemed like the wise answer of a calculated politician.

It took a long time for DeSantis to make up his mind, I wonder if he was willing to commit himself. Was he a procrastinator or did his cold feet get the better of him? He threw his hat in the ring, and only he knew if that was the right call at the right time. Was he ready to be commander in chief? Did he have the character and fortitude? Was he pushed, coaxed, and cajoled to jump into the race?

Unfortunately, DeSantis had not made the important transition from local state governorship to a potential national leader. His failed Twitter launch seemed to be an omen for his standing in the race. His COVID success and anti-vaccination, anti-lockdown rhetoric did not gather much traction as an indication of astute and shrewd leadership beyond the borders of Florida. DeSantis had everything going for him. He wanted to make his mark in politics and be one of the political stalwarts of our time. The leadership of the Republican Party was given to him on a platter, but he chose "not to mellow."

Many issues dogged Ron's presidential bid:

1. He did not give a careful and deep analysis of the GOP's transition away from a traditional and conformist political

party. He did not have a strong personality, although his political demise was not a personality issue.

2. He did not fully understand what a majority of the Republican base had become under Trump. They had become more non-conformist and not the world, interpreted, they think independently.

3. Ron thought his popularity in Florida could translate into national success.

4. Ron underestimated Trump's influence and hold on the Republican Party.

5. Ron became complacent and was not sharp or shrewd enough to develop a better political strategy rather than relying on his past successes. Among other problems, many people found him to be awkward and uncharismatic. A high degree of lukewarmness was standing in his way. His lack of political experience and strategy were quite evident.

Given the challenges that come with being a successful politician, was DeSantis ever up to the test of being a presidential candidate, or was he just a forced ripe Florida orange? If he had successfully overcome these challenges he would be the Republican nominee.

Not Another Novice
The need of a Republican
Pedigree and Thoroughbred

The profile of a novice is obvious, and the telltale signs were clear from the first words uttered in the 2016 campaign. The tone, backdrop, and future of the Trump presidency was set. With patience and unwavering faith that would "take them to heaven, if possible," Trump's ardent supporters, media personalities, and political allies believed with all their hearts that he would rise to the level of an elder statesman and ultimately become presidential, considering the gravity of the office being held. Many had hoped that the inflamed heart and thirst for hate and bigotry would be quenched. He would strike a balance and calm social and political anxieties and fears. Their faith was dashed, and their hopes and dreams did not come to fruition—but they would prefer to bury their heads in the sand. Trump has thrived from birth with a privileged mentality, treats everybody as tools or toys to satisfy his whims.

The bigwigs in the GOP are incapable of saving themselves. They seem to not want to be saved. They mope around Congress and their constituents as lost souls. It is difficult to see hearts and minds wasted as Donald Trump rakes the party and its members over hot coals. Some seem not to mind being raked. Many are willing to offer themselves as sacrifices to the cult that is an albatross around the neck of the GOP.

Many pay lip service, but in their hearts, they want to get rid of the "scorcher, the hot bonnet pepper" Trump. The GOP needs to be saved from itself. They do not need another novice. At this important juncture, there is a dire need for a Republican thoroughbred with GOP pedigree to put the GOP back on a path of political relevance and patriotism.

In today's GOP circus, many do not understand the responsibility and purpose of the Republican Party. The GOP is under a complex spiritual attack from within and without, subverting and repressing its true purpose. The party needs a specialist to steer it out of its present political mess. I am tempted to look back at the glorious moral and spiritual heights from which the GOP has fallen.

The Republican Party was the progenitor of political purpose, national pride, and godly direction. The Republican Party chose to establish a high moral ground on which the pillars of the American state now stands. The early Republicans, with Abraham Lincoln as its leader, chose practicality and sound judgement to keep the union together rather than having states splintering and seceding from the union. The Republican leadership then, described slavery as "a crisis of conscience," which propelled the party to take a stand against the expansion of slavery in other states. Many Southerners, Democrats, businessmen, and slave owners lacked ethics and a moral compass and did not see anything wrong with enslaving other human beings. The agrarian economy, slavery, the slave trade, and international markets were in sync. They fed off each other in perfect harmony to bring profits to Europe and America.

The Industrial Revolution, the invention of the cotton gin, and the rise of sugarcane, the "green gold" generated high demand in the international markets. The American South was basking in the glow and "sweet spot of slavery." It was supplying local and international markets with sugar and cotton. They thought it would be economic suicide to end slavery since it was the lifeblood of Southern economy.

The Republicans had a higher perception, discernment, and insight into human and moral relations. They were ethically more evolved and advanced, and they had a loftier viewpoint of the true purpose of their fellow human beings and how they should be treated. Although slavery was the economic engine that provided wealth for the South with its large plantations, Republican leaders saw the many negatives brought about by slavery. The consequences, exploitation, and inhumane treatment of slaves included castration, whipping, branding, amputation, sexual assault and abuse. Deep racial divisions impacted the lives of slaves, families and communities. Slavery had an even stronger negative impact. The development of industries stalled because of slavery and the slave-driven economy. The technological advances sweeping parts of Europe and the North were not welcomed in the American south.

The early Republican leaders were up against many moral, social, political, and economic obstacles, but they persisted. They could not be bought or sold, dissuaded or distracted, because they were the real deal. They understood their true calling. They were not in a crisis mode or a do-nothing mode. Their pride, commitment, political objective and calling was to be true to themselves and their party. They would not allow the brutality of slavery to spread to other states, rendering the new American democracy a republic of barbarity.

In 1860, Republicans espoused a spirit of duty and obligation to the call of godly principle and purpose on which the United States was built. They had clean, clear, and unsmeared consciences. Their language and tone spoke volumes about their vision for a place where prosperity, innovation, and dreams could become a reality. They were firmly planted on the truth of God, human rights, and justice for all. These men were not stumbling blocks or knuckleheads, and their choice of words and intent were unwavering.

The 1860 Republican Convention Platform

"We the delegated representatives of the Republican electors of the United States in convention assembled, in discharged of the duty we owe to our constituents and our country, unite in declaring:

1. The Republican causes are permanent, a necessary and perpetual part of the United States, history and constitutional success.
2. That the principles outlined in the declaration of independence and the federal Constitution is essential to the preservation of the United State republic and its institutions:
   a) All men are created equal,
   b) All men are endowed by their creator with certain inalienable rights, to life, liberty and the pursuit of happiness. Further stated, to secure these rights, governments are instituted, with the consent of the governed, which is essential to the preservation of the republic's institutions, federal constitutions and state rights.
3. That the people are indebted to the United States, its material resources, its rapid augmentation of wealth, its development, honor at home and abroad, we therefore hold in abhorrence all schemes for disunion, from any source.

It's beyond the scope of reality of what we are experiencing in today's Republicans. They have completely flipped what the Republican Party is all about. The Democrats have taken up the mantle for stability, disunion and anti-chaos.

The dizzying heights of purpose, sound judgment, and political astuteness from which the current GOP leadership has fallen should be an indictment for betrayal of trust and purpose.

In an advanced and increasingly threatening world, there is an urgent need for a Republican thoroughbred with true Republican pedigree. There is no place or need for political gamesmanship or gimmicks in words and deeds. This Republican thoroughbred should understand the gravity of the presidential office and be an inspiration for good. He should have the backbone to carry the weight of the office and the mental capacity and acuity to understand societies, ethnic groups, races, economics, history, religion, the past, present, and a vision for the future. This prospective commander in chief will value the sacrifices of lives lost and maimed through military combat and should earn the respect and honor of those in harm's way.

A communicator and commander in chief that demand attention and respect at home and abroad. This articulate negotiator needs a balanced perspective and must be spiritually grounded. This individual does not need to be a Republican clone, but he must understand and know what it means to be a true Republican.

PART II
Poems, Politics, and Prose

An Epic Election

An election like this you will never again experience,
In this lifetime or the next,
Totally consuming, extraordinarily epic.
At the epicenter of the referendum is a stable genius, an amazing human specimen,
A character and personality of rare mental faculties and psychological traits,
A master of reverse psychology and name-tagging.
He appears in human form only once in a hundred years,
Born and bred for a time as this, with innate skills to manipulate, beguile, hypnotize,
Enchant, and mesmerize.

A mastermind, armed with deftness, stealthiness of hand and mind,
In four short years, he stepped out of the legislature and the federal government,
Back pedal from Congress and the RNC and unto his own throne,
Forcing the knees and backs of almost every distracting senator in his party,
compelling them to bow, to fall in line with his massive adulating base,
a savior-seeking throng, wide-eyed with unquenchable thirst for a white messiah.
Judicial apparatus and puppets, political instruments he set in place to
Move his agenda to the next level, positioning heads of departments to be his foot soldiers

In his pockets are bodies and minds, ever-forgiving souls, eager and ready to do his bidding,
Surmising that they were left out, hung to dry by Obama, the previous light bearer.

The demons and serpents in their hearts and minds, the half-white
"melanin king" never did
Crush, now this precious election cycle they can't afford to blink
or miss a beat,
Their only bind, their white messiah's penchant for frivolousness,
His irascible and erratic deportment is stifling, his infection from
the dreaded foot-in-mouth disease, His never-ending bait and
switch, further arouse anxiety and nervousness in his base,
Levels of human passion and emotions rise, every passing day the
stakes grow higher,
Wrapped up in their franchises, a single piece of ballot, representing
a precious ideal, a
Republic that understands and feels, will we win or will we all
lose, now is the time to
Choose, will there be a statement, will there be a strong message
sent like an earthquake?
From the tip of Florida to Alaska, Trump is king,
Will there be a reprimand of the state of affairs.

After the storm and the dogfight, with billions of dollars spent,
Will political capital and hard earned currency be wasted or
gained?
Every corner of the earth will know, this will not be Forgotten,
In the year 2024, the sound will be heard, at midnight, on
November 5.

Waiting for the Election Verdict

What will be the verdict?
While the ship sailed the stormy seas, was the captain clearheaded or drunk,
overwhelmed by the turbulence and the tide,
was he sleeping at the helm or was he on the john with his fingers twitching?

Narratives, crude and divisive, remarks caustic and course,
inflaming passions of division and strife, awakening sleeping clans,
tribes, and armed fractions, like insects, they are emboldened,
crawling out of the woodwork, bereft of compassion, empathy or care.

Where is the moral compass when it is needed most? We have lost our footing,
moral authority and clout. Ethics trampled, caution thrown to the wind.
When will the calming voices with words of sanity speak? Will common sense prevail? I am impatiently waiting for the verdict.

We have been through stormy weather before, navigated many rocky shores in the darkest of night, but we came together as a unit, beating many difficult odds. Our vibrating pedestal is cracked. Lady Liberty seems to be falling. American democracy is now on the ballot.

Is this the mighty eagle decimated by personality politics? Will health care lose its dynamism,
Science and technology its cutting edge? Will common logic and wisdom give way to buffoonery and horse crap? Will third world antics and chicanery replace professionalism and diplomacy? Will the politics of division and strife make a mockery of democracy? Will national pride take a hit?

I am waiting for the verdict. It will be interesting to see if the republic will continue to cannibalize itself. Will loyalty and true patriotism—the hope and lifeblood of a nation—continue to be replaced by self-serving demagogues. Are they sucking dry the American dream with fear and despair? What will the verdict be?

The founding fathers, war heroes, and civil rights leaders must be turning in their graves like spindles on a shaft to see that the sacrifices they made are being trampled on and dragged in the mud. With insight and vision, they put in place the cornerstones of the Constitution written in blood, to preserve the social fabric and propel the union to the epitome of human achievement through continuous advancement.

Shortsighted and heedless brains—as empty as space—twist and turn the nuts and bolts to loosen and backtrack to an era of darkness and pain. Many are drawn to narcissism and bigotry like moths to a flame, others are forced to contend that their lives matter at a moment like this.

Evangelicals are blind, deaf, and dumb.
They are playing the clown while praying and prophesying amiss.
Will the impartial light of grace shine through?
We will all see. I am waiting for the verdict.

"Donald, Don't Throw It All Away"

Don, don't throw it all away.
Prove them wrong.
The stable genius that you are,
Your reputation will be on the line,
Your legacy will be sullied, soiled, and marred,
They would want to rub it in your face like tar.

Don, don't throw it all away.
The strong faith they pour into you,
Over eighty million votes strong, political capital at your disposal.
Pull the ills together, mend the divide.
Some wish that you would slip and slide.

Like a physician, others look to you to heal,
The political sores, the economic bleed.
Don, don't throw it all away.
The American democracy is depending on you.

Strengthen the Republican caucus, the Republican vote,
Do it twice, for the Grand Ole Party.
Get it done in the second term.
Don, don't throw it all away.
Bite your lip and hold your tongue.
Pause the Twitter fingers, show fortitude and strength,
Silence the critics, let them eat their words,
Let them swallow their liberal pride.

The prophets of doom and the distractions,
Prove them wrong.
Don, many are depending on you.
You are the white hope.
Before you make your move,
Think twice and don't throw it all away.

Many have gone the way of QAnon,
They have turned to conspiracy theories,
Party fringes, and paramilitary groups.
One interpretation is the MAGA cult.
Another is admiration and affection,
Die-hardness and homage.

They need a messiah and a shepherd.
Like sheep, many have gone away.
Pull them from the path of self-defeat and destruction,
To the path of objectivity and truth.

It's all up to you now, Don.
Don't throw it all away.
Lead them or drive them astray.

Ode to Joe, Sleepy Joe Awakes

Many thought he was washed up, down and out.
Ridiculed for his age and stutter, few praise him or flatter.
His opponents took nasty swipes at him, few encouraged him.
Some made corny jokes, punctuated with laugher, bad-mouthed and berated him,
Name-tagged him, "Sleepy Joe," subtly belittling his intelligence, stamina, acuity, and acumen.

Slow and steady, Joe rises to the occasion. Now the gloves are off.
Like a champion, he bounces around with pep in his steps and renewed vigor.
He smells blood, a certain color scalp he is hunting. "Mister, I am awake, I have what it takes
I am coming for you,"

They thought they should have him admitted to the geriatric or gerontology center.
To their surprise, he has outmaneuvered their traps and flops. Dirt and slime they threw, injecting bitterness to soil his character.
They tried to discount and defame,
Mr. President will never be added to his name.

Evangelicals and men of faith, false prophets, and daydreamers had a field day.
They bet that God would anoint and choose a pussy grabber over a collected brain and a humble soul. Now Joe, as nimble as a cat and as sly as a fox, moves and steps like the Matrix, in the pics,
Calm and collected, measured and substantive. With gravity and clout, a confident swagger,
Poise and experience, vision and foresight,
Emotional intellect, fraught with compassion and graciousness,
Joe has found his voice, command, and style.
"I'm no young chicken, but I know a lot."

The tables have been turned. The attempt to steal his thunder has failed.

They tried to cramp his style painted him as naive and weak.

They can't see the giant or the strength of steel under the hood.

To their surprise, Joe is now wide-awake. His shades are on, and his stutter is gone.

Look Before You Leap

A destructive and wicked act,
Off the ground, in no time you are airborne, leaping,
Now midway in the leap, your mind's eye is refocusing.
You are now wondering what's ahead of you,
What you are landing yourself into.
Regrets, conscience, beating, and biting,
Self-inflicted stress, strain, and defeat.
May God help you, but you should have looked.

The noise from inside your soul is deafening, unbearable.
"I should have looked before I leaped."
It's much more than crossing an intersection or a busy street.
It's processing your action,
Premeditating on your decisions.
It's a mental exercise, a process, scouting and investigating,
Looking for the pros and the cons,
The good and the bad of what you are getting yourself into.

Preparing for the act, ready for the jump,
Your mind is set, determination is at the fore.
Behavior is jumpy, first wait a bit,
Lose some steam, evaluate the impulsive action.
Bounce it around a little, juggle it in your head.

This may be an important action
So be patient before you act.
Once you have jumped, there is no turning back,
No time to evaluate, you would have already jumped.

"Time is too short," you say. "No time to look, I have to jump,
I don't care where I land, In a pig pen or quick sand,"
A blind jump you take. What is beneath the sod?
You will not know until you have landed.

The mess you make, you have to own it
For your own good and peace of mind, unearth the traps.
Cross-examine and double-check. Discover the truths before you leap.
Do that before you make your move.

Whatsoever is at stake—that's the choice you make.
A nonchalant leap you take—prepare for your fate.
Look before you leap, unless by faith, a blind leap you take.
You are leaping with God.

Sun Dodge, Climate Change

I was in love with the sun—but not like before.
A sun worshiper was I,
There were times when I would frolic and fun,
Without shade, in the heat of the sun.
It always gives me energy, a sign of life and hope.
Sun, seeing you rise was a lovely treat.
A sign of freedom, independence, creativity, and new beginnings.

Now things and times have changed.
I dodge the sun when I can, if I can.
We are now all out of love.
I now prefer precipitation, moisture, and vapor.
I love the mist and the fog,
Dark days and clouds of gray.
Dew on the ground and droplets of rain,
Beating down on my forehead and on my face.
I prefer the tingle of cold rainwater,
Soaking through my pants and shirt.

They say, "Sun, you've gone bad."
They say you are getting worse every day.
You are penetrating the mesosphere,
Entering the stratosphere as raw as ever.
Right through the troposphere, where we live,
With burning heat, a deadly vengeance, pent-up rage.

Here, where we live in the atmosphere,
Chemicals and aerosols damage the earth's layers.
The frequent charcoal and garbage burning.
Fuel and carbon emissions, gases and chemical substances.

Smoke particles and pollutants going up into the clouds,
Coming down on us as acid rain.
All these impair and damage the protective layer.
Scientists call it the ozone layer.

Now, old sun, your hot, destructive rays cannot
Be strained or contained.
They are making wide holes in the natural strainer, the ozone
layer.
The miles-wide holes are getting bigger,
Because pollutants are going up with more vigor,
Causing a greenhouse effect.
It's like being trapped in a hothouse.
So, the climate is changing, the weather is now dramatic,
Acting topsy-turvy.

The delicate ice shelves are melting,
Unbalancing the climates and the tides, the weather pattern and
seasons.
Mother Nature is moaning,
Her wildlife is sweating and crying.
Her wetlands are drying, and coral reefs are bleaching.
The hurricanes are packing more punches,
Wildfires and destructive tornadoes.
I wish to betray my stupid hunches,
Are my todays my good old days?

You lucky old sun, I still like you,
But things and times have changed.
Now I prefer precipitation, the cold and the wet.
The droplets and the rain, the mist and the fog,
The clouds and days of gray
The stupid paradox of the sun.

Scientists say, because of you, lucky old sun, or us,
The counts of sperm in men are getting lower.
You have more far-reaching effects than we can ever imagine.
You are even making us much slower with less power.

Important vitamin D you give, yes.
They say you are not like before.
Now things have changed.
The protection that was installed, your guard, our defense,
It's disappearing.
I dodge the sun—when and if I can.

Where Your Mind Is

That's what you get.
Your ambition and dreams are where your mind is.
Your hopes and determination,
Your contemplation is in your mind.
Your mind is in your thoughts and dreams.
Your dreams will carry you, support you, and transport you.

The sense of inferiority and inadequacy,
Self-confidence and achievement.
The mind is where the concept is conceived,
Where the ray of hope is seen.
Where attitude, strength and ability are exercised,
Nourished, and grown.
Success and accomplishment are achieved,
Self-doubt and defeat are realized where the mind is.

You are going where your mind is.
The road you are traveling on.
You have been there—where your mind is.

That's what you see, what you conceive and believe.
You get valuable support.
You start to build where the mind is.
The complex begins, inferiority or superiority,
Insecurity or security, conditioning and adjustment.
Manipulation and malfunction,
Cybernetics and control begin and end where your mind is.

The seat of personal privacy,
Your own sacred space.
No blood or tissue,
The I am that you are,
The invisible you that can make or break you.

It's up to you and no one else,
To put strength and determination where your mind is.
The decision and common sense, to work smarter or harder,
Let your mind solve the problem.
Finding the solution—not part of the problem.
Nothing can compensate.
Use it as a tool.
A genius or a fool is where your mind is.

Andrae Powell

The Shallowness

It's a bore,
Where all the mess is.
Shattered pieces, debris, and waste wash ashore,
Squalor, filth, and impurities gather galore,
In the shallowness of the shore.

Lack of depth, not enough space causes bruises and sore,
Nothing much to see and explore.
Prepare yourself to be messed up amid the mess and the filth,
The impurities that gather and store
In the shallowness of the shore.

The shallowness is where the masses love to wallow,
Here they meddle and dabble,
Spending most of their talent and interest,
Their lifetime and energy.
They find what they are looking for.
In the shallowness of the shore.

It's a personal decision that is made,
To stay and stray in the shallowness.
A cheap price to pay, little or nothing,
Hardly a sacrifice.

Too much to encounter beyond this periphery,
So, they would rather sit in the froth and stare at the scum that
around them gather.
Soon they will be a part of the filth and the waste,
A member of the inhabitants of the shallow

I must vacate, swim, or dive,
I am not prepared to be part of the shit, poop, and crap.
I don't want to be messed up among the scum and the waste.

I must relocate, remove myself from the monotony,
The bore, and the turbulence of the tide.
That batter and bruise the shallowness and the shore,
With its constant ebb and flow, ebb and flow.
The eternal splashing and beating,
The nagging shells, here the sands are not ready,
Not prepared to turn into pearls.
Careless pebbles, sometimes jagged edge, lazy rocks,
Like stilettoes waiting to batter and bruise and sometimes kill.

The pandemonium of the shallowness,
Uprooting seaweed and delicacies of the seabed.
Morning noon and night, the never-ending confusion,
The endless erosion.

The shallowness can only dispense what it's got,
Confusion and madness, no discipline or order.
No sense of purpose, uniformity, or control.
The grime mixed with sand and dirt and shit bags.

Froth mixed with scum bags.
Everything, everyone, doing their own thing, trying to move,
To prove, to stay alive, they don't know,
There is no reshaping, resetting, or retiring,
It's the damn shallowness.
Here the waves do nothing but batter, disrupt, and erupt,
Pounding the shallow and the shore,
Making its inhabitants out of order and insipid.
Displaying a behavior of unbelief and utter disgust.

Got to get out of this mode,
The wearing and the tearing,
The constant eroding and misbehavior.

The contemptuous shallowness can be forgiven,
But not when there is the big wide ocean and depth, for cleansing,
To conquer and discover.
The enormous space, peace and tranquility,
Where all the beauty and wealth are stored.
The shallowness seems alluring,
The depth seems perilous and precarious,
But it's the deep that propels curiosity,
Stirs imagination, the wealth of inspiration,
Opens the mind and makes you aware,
Unlocking your latent powers.

The shallowness keeps you frustrated,
Threatening to blow your top, short circuit your fuse,
Driving you crazy while unscrewing your bolts
With its restlessness and disorder,
Eroding your mental, physical, and spiritual faculties.
There might be danger out there in the deep,
But that's how I learn and become smarter.

I prefer the deep and what it has to offer,
Instead of the subtle and deceptive traps of the shallow.
The deep is for launching and wonder,
Amazement and thrill, cleansing and rejuvenation,
Presenting to you what life is all about.
The deep is a reverse of the agitation,
The turmoil and commotion,
The flip side of disarray and discord
That gathers in the shallowness of the shore.

Fermenting

Living matter and substances,
Decay and change,
Physical and chemical reaction,
Good to bad and vice versa.

It might be for better or worse.
What the outcome will be I don't know as yet.
I only see it and smell it.

The momentum is gathering,
The process has begun, we are in the making.
The heat and chemical reaction,
The pressure is building, everything is swelling.
Already acidic, pungent odors rising,
The color schemes of things are changing.
The axis of evil and homegrown terrorists,
Nukes and bombs.
Israel and Palestine, Hezbollah, Hamas, and the Houthis.
Iranian and Syrian fixation, the North Korean brain-sick,
The Middle East mindset on the disintegration of Israel.

Fossil fuels and global warming,
Erratic temperature changes and natural disasters.
The EU and one world order,
Russian hacking and aggression,
Poisoning and killing its dissidents.
Bombing and obliterating Ukraine

Moral decay and suicide,
The rise and fall of nations,
The red dragon and the rest.

Good wine or bad,
Like fruits and sugarcane,
Vinegar or grapes on the vine.
Sour, bitter, or sweet, the effervescence is stifling
The environmental conditions are perfect,
The breakdown and changes.
The environment is not cool, it's too hot for preservation.

We are fermenting.
Father Time is working overtime for us.
We are pushing it over the limit.
Transportation and prices, housing and development,
Gas prices and politics, education and social unrest,
East-West agitation and natural disasters,
The brew is frightening.
We are fermenting.
I wish the gut feelings would betray me,
I'll have to wait and see the end of this process.
Wonder what it's turning out to be.
All this heat and changes,
A new dawn might be on the horizon.

Blistering Sores Metastasizing into Cancerous Lesions

The blistering sores of race relations have now become infected.
The thought of a systematic infection is now seen as an open wound.
Like salt in an open wound, careless words and actions bring tears to eyes and pain to hearts.
Racial inequalities, disparities, and tension,
Invoked by a pandemic, bring memories of the oppressed,
Dormant, battered, bruised, and wounded spirits come to life,
Blistering sores now metastasizing into cancerous lesions.

Viewed as systemic, some see cultural dissimilarities.
Others see racial hatred and bitterness,
Always a simmering dormant issue.
Many see decades of oppressed spirits, shackled by chains of hate,
Misunderstanding and fear, in a cycle of injustice,
Metastasizing into social cancerous lesions.

Blistering sores of division and strife, perpetuated by political tribalism,
Reshape hearts and minds, expose wounds of hate and deep-rooted fear.
Fuel keeps adding to the fire of hate.
In spite of the hope for positive actions to heal and alleviate,
The Holy-Mary-Thank-You Jesus moment will not come.

You were made to believe that modern times would bring days of enlightenment.
The days of enlightenment are getting darker than before.
Working behind the scenes, agents and operatives are sharpening tools for political castration,
With un-sanitized hands and hearts and a bankrupt mentality, they make a bad situation worse.

COVID Money: The Stink
and Shame of the PPP

It's like illegal sex,
Abuse of the disadvantaged, the haves raping the have-nots.
Robbing the paycheck-to-paycheck earners,
Taking their little from the pot.
Can't bear to see someone else's fruit on the tree without picking it,
Even though their barns are fat—and their storerooms are full.

It's goes up to karma as a shameful sight and a stinking smell,
Karma has no eyes, so it cannot see,
It only feels and knows what should and should not be.
Like when the trade wars started with the Chinese, they had to find a virus.
They say, "To hell with them—so let it be."

Earmarked and framed to soothe the pain and discomfort of the hobbled,
To appease the suffering from the COVID ills.
With the backing of financiers, brokers, and bankers,
Like ravenous wolves and hungry sharks,
They descended on the PPP.

Evangelicals, False Hopes, and False Prophets

What has become of Evangelicals?
They defy true interpretation and definition.
Are they Christians? Are they evangelists, apologists, or defenders
of Protestantism?
It seems confusing. What is their true calling?
Do they evangelize the infidels and the outcasts?
Do they bring the spiritually wounded, the lost and dying sheep,
to the fold?
Do they have a passion for souls?
Do they think some people are not worthy of redemption by the
blood of Jesus, or God's saving grace?
Are they Zealous to spread the good news, "Jesus Saves"?
Do they choose to clothe the naked and feed the hungry,
The motherless and the sick—or are they political armor-bearers?

From the outside looking in, it seems as if Evangelicals are now
hardcore,
Spiritual revelers and rebels, wrapped in the garments of
Christianity,
Promoting political agendas. Like tumbleweeds, they roll around
in the winds of change on Satan's politically parched, dry desert,
kicking themselves against the pricks while making fools of
themselves.
If they are indeed genuine, they need to return the MAGA caps,
dust off their Bibles,
Seek the will and face of God instead of the will and desires of
Trump and his worship of the God of Mammon.

Some people believe Evangelicals are spiritual white supremacists
and Klansmen,
Clothed in prophetic and biblical garb, spirituality, and religion.
They seem to want to tell God what to do because he doesn't
know the heart and mentality of a pussy grabber. They forgot

what God said to Samuel: "Men look at the outward appearance,
but the Lord looks at the heart." They seem to want to force the
hand of God,
They are convinced that God is color-blind.
They are intent on wrapping God around their bird brains and
finite mentalities.
For this, they must put themselves to shame, making spiritual
things a laughingstock,
Spreading false claims like wildfire.

They swore on the Bible and on smelly graves that God gave them
a word.
That God told them that He prefers chaos over order,
God told them that chaos will reign. "Close the drawbridge and
trickle down the economy,
Turn your backs on the poor, the hungry, the motherless, and the
dying,
Give the children's bread to the dogs, their meat to the trash bin."
Why would they want to swear that God spoke to them?
If you say God said it—but he never did—it's a spiritual preemptive
strike.
People will get hurt.

Don't be fooled. Prayers were prayed and answered, and the
outcome was already decided. He had already given the electoral
victory. Trump's good deeds were eternally documented, but the
incumbent kept interjecting himself. He kept stealing the glory,
coveting all praise and honor,
Beating his chest until it was black and blue. How long would you
expect God to put up with someone Who keeps making a mess
and stepping in it?

Affluenza Kids Playing Seditious Selfish Games

It can be a real mess when affluenza kids grow up and want to function in a normal world with all their abnormalities. When it comes to politics, it's even more bizarre, mind-boggling, and devious. It's like the circus comes to town. You see and hear things, and you wonder out load, "Is this an open season for craziness?"
The line has been crossed. After decades of a proficient electoral process,
Success, and stability in national elections, here comes the affluenza kid.
The wannabe strongman's sole intent is to self-serve, democracy to breach.

Affluenza kids, deprived of inadequate positive mental stimulation, are unpredictable.
As grown men, they ply their irrationality and irresponsibility on the national and world stage.
With power in their grip, you might think they would exhibit some degree of democratic pride, decorum, normalcy, restraint, maturity, and grace, political protocols demand, even in "shithole countries," they rise to the occasion of leadership. They accept a loss after all legal avenues have been explored, bow out gracefully, call a spade a spade, build and repair legacies, and do what normal political opponents do. They show strength of character despite a loss. In good faith and grace, they take the trashing and congratulate their opponents for a well-fought fight.

Affluenza kids, now grown adults, show no signs of maturity. They roll over on their backs, kick their feet stubbornly in the air and expose their underbellies. Their minds are ingrained in entitlement. They think everyone should bow to their whims, hogwash, and incoherent bull.
Things should go their way, and if they don't, expect a temper tantrum or retribution.

They want to slash and burn the barn, put to waste the corn, and
spill the milk.
They will open the door of the coop to let the foxes in, if their
needs are not met
They think everything should be given to them on a platter.

Everyone should scramble to satisfy their affluence and powder
their warped egos.
Their opioid is constant praise and adulation. They need to be
petted and flattered.
They are not anchored in reality. The important lessons in life
they have not learned.
They are always festering in grievances and fights.
In the real world, things don't work out as planned.
As a result, they will always be chasing the wind.

So, you thought the electorate had spoken? When all is said and
done,
Results are not in their favor, things don't go as anticipated.
With affluenza adults, this cannot be possible. A o, is unacceptable,
Everything must be given to them. The word no, is not a part of
their vocabulary.
They were bred in an environment that was secluded from the
real world,
Their actions should have no consequences, they think they should
do as they please.

After the dead end of politics is reached, with no recourse,
They toy with seditious games, they pit democracy against itself,
The courts and the justice system in a meltdown, Senators against
Senators.
Instead of conceding to their opponents, they prefer to demonize,
spread confusion and hate,
Ply conspiracy theories, drag the political process in the mud.
They did not get their shiny toy, they kidnap the political system,

hold it in bondage, and display a fit of "adult affluenza paralysis."
Not satisfied with judicial and the electoral recourse, they
employ seditious games, invite anarchy, tumult and turmoil, send
threats of sadness and woe,
Judgement and disaster, doom and gloom, let society cannibalize
itself.

Retreat

Retreat, take a break, get away,
Re-energize and live to fight another day.
You need to retreat,
Take a day or two off and some time out.
Disappear, hide away, hide out,
Take time out, de-stress your mind, and clear your head.
A few days' rest, plain and simple,
relax, forget about the income tax.

Take it easy, find the river or a stream
The ocean or the sea.
Let the sea breeze blow in your face and eyes.
Let it absorb and take the depression, the stress and frustrations.
Get in the water, dogpaddle off some of the weight.
Don't drown yourself—refresh your soul.

Too much mental load carrying, eyes burning, brain frying,
Like an overloaded lorry, this will break you down in no time.
It only needs your blood pressure to go up a notch or two—and
that's it!
A stroke or cardiac arrest.
Permanent damage to yourself.
Who can you blame? Who will bear your pain?
No one will step forward or say,
"Let me for you, your pain to bear."
They will pass you sitting or lying there,
Giving you only their tired and worn-out stare.
They don't even B.S. care.

Too much weight on your mind and nerves.
Retreat, it's good for you.
Flush yourself, eliminate the toxic and unwanted thoughts,
People, and events clogging your mind and mental faculties.

The phones and laptop, the papers and the schedules,
Put them aside for a while.
Smarten up and be wise.
Don't run yourself into the ground—
Or burn yourself out.

Smell the roses while you can,
Take a walk in the park, appreciate the life you have
Retreat, get out of your own way, and get away.
Back off, beat it, delete and retreat.

Andrae Powell

Smell

The best thing you can do for you,
Is to guard and protect your smell.
Your mouth and body, head-to-foot smell,
Some will be brave enough to you, they tell,
That you smell very repulsive and obnoxious,
Some will not.
Others will hold their breath,
Not to inhale but to expel your smell.

We all love to take a whiff,
But only great fragrances and sweet smells.
Delicious fruity and heavenly scents,
Not the foul, stinking hell smell,
Stale body odor and bad breath.
Around you, no one will dwell or behave well.
They will twist and turn while you are talking,
Scratching and itching, while you are not noticing.
Trying to hide it, not making it obvious to you,
That something is seriously wrong,
While pretending that all is well.
And that they are with you, uncomfortable as hell.
They are playing stink games with you, but you can't tell.

In your eyes, with you, they are laughing and smiling,
You are there beside them, and in their faces,
Protruding and producing all that stink odor and smell.
Thinking all is well,
But in their minds, they are vomiting as hell.
They are terribly distracted by your smell.

Before you leave the house,
To get in your car or on the bus,
On the street or appear in the public's eye,
Forget the time and the rush, make it a habit.
Check your breath, body odor, and personal hygiene.
Your mouth and gum, dental hygiene and smile.
Your grooming, don't forget, clean or shine your shoes,
Check your pants and shirt, your blouse and skirt.
Back and front, your pubic tits, and armpits.

Friends and loved ones, sweethearts and adoring fans,
They will be kissing and hugging, smelling and touching you.
Strangers will be passing, coming and going,
Moving, bouncing around, crashing into you.
You are there, ranting and raving,
Smiling and flirting, dancing or talking,

Smiling and having the time of your life.
They will be orbiting you like the sun.

Thinking all is well, you are swinging like a million dollars.
Feeling all cute and fancy, pretty or handsome, feeling swell,
The life of the party.
Unknown to you, others are very much turned off by you.
Disturbed by your offensive smell.
Perturbed and agitated, stunned and disgusted by your foul smell.

You've got to be confident about your teeth, your mouth, and laughter,
Your head, hair, and underarm smell.
Once you are ready and out of the house, you are on the go.
Make sure your appearance and smell are not the last thing on your mind.

You've got to guard and protect your smell.
It might be nutrition or glands,
They don't know, and they don't care.
It's best not to embarrass yourself,
Or cause anyone to be offended by your smell.

Make sure when it's in someone else's direction,
It's good heavenly scent.
If not, stay by yourself.